It's NATURE!

S E R I E S

Weird Walkers

12 OF NATURE'S
MOST AMAZING ANIMALS

by Anthony D. Fredericks

NorthWord Press
Minnetonka, Minnesota
www.howtobookstore.com

DEDICATION

For my son Jonathan—

with love and admiration.

ACKNOWLEDGMENTS

Special thanks to Mary Fitzgibbons—librarian at the Dover Area Community Library— whose unfailing assistance and engaging effervescence made this book a reality.

Photography © 1996 by: Kitchin & Hurst/Tom Stack & Associates, Front Cover; Mark J. Thomas/Dembinsky Photo Associates, 3; Darrell Gulin/Dembinsky Photo Associates, 4; Jim Brandenburg/Minden Pictures, 5, 19; Norbert Wu/www.norbertwu.com, 7, 28; Skip Moody/ Dembinsky Photo Associates, 9; Art Wolfe, 11; Beverly Joubert/National Geographic Image Collection, 13, 22; Ken Davis/Tom Stack & Associates, 15; R. F. Ashley/Visuals Unlimited, 17; Bill Curtsinger, 21 top; David B. Fleetham/Pacific Stock, 21 bottom; Tim Laman, 24; Gary Mezaros/Dembinsky Photo Associates, 27; James P. Blair/National Geographic Image Collection, 31.

NorthWord Press
5900 Green Oak Drive
Minnetonka, MN 54343
1-800-328-3895
www.howtobookstore.com

Illustrations by Kay Povelite
Book design by Lisa Moore

ISBN 1-55971-630-4

Printed in Malaysia
10 9 8 7 6 5 4 3 2 1

WEIRD WALKERS

CONTENTS

Ostrich

About Walkers

Starfish

How do you walk? Like many people, you put one foot in front of the other, lift the back foot, and move it ahead of the one on the ground. Then you repeat the action. The motion is not complex.

It's something you do every day. It's also an efficient way of getting from one place to another.

Mangrove trees

Walking is a form of locomotion (or travel) that allows an organism, such as yourself, to move through its environment. The distance traveled may be a few inches a day or many miles a week. Many species use walking as a way to search for food, to seek shelter, or to locate potential mates for breeding. Some species combine walking with other forms of locomotion such as running, flying, or swimming. How and why an organism walks is related to its lifestyle and its survival needs. Many organisms have specialized forms of walking that make them unique. Some organisms can walk straight up trees. Other organisms can walk backward. A few can walk upside down. There is an incredible number of walking methods, each different from the way *you* typically walk.

In this book you will discover some of the most unusual walkers on our planet. You'll learn about a fish that walks *out* of the water, a lizard that walks *on* the water, and even a tree that "walks" *through* the water. As you read, think about how these forms of locomotion are similar to, or different from, the way you walk, skip, or run. How and where an organism walks is part of how it has been able to adapt to its environment. You will be surprised to discover that the act of walking, for many organisms, may be more complex than you originally thought.

Mudskippers are members of the Goby family, a group of fish whose pectoral fins are shaped like suckers—allowing them to cling to rocks and other slippery surfaces. Mudskippers live in mangrove swamps and mudflats from West Africa to Southeast Asia and the Southwest Pacific Ocean. They range from 5 to 12 inches long and look like tadpoles with very large heads. Their "pop-eyes" are their most distinctive physical feature.

Startling Steppers

When we think of fish, we usually think about creatures that glide through the ocean or swim in a lake. But there's one fish that spends most of its time out of water and, oddly enough, most of its time climbing trees—it's the mudskipper.

This unique fish has specially developed fins which allow it to walk across the mudflats of seashores and rivers and climb up the trunks of mangrove trees. The **pectoral fins** are on the front of the mudskipper. They are very large and are similar to the limbs of a land animal. The **pelvic fins** are on the back of this fish. They are joined together to form a modified sucker used for grasping limbs and branches.

Although it's an ocean creature, the mudskipper frequently swims to shore. There, it leaps onto the beach and begins to walk by pulling itself along with its front fins. This walking motion makes it look like a miniature seal. An entire school of mudskippers "walking" along the shoreline is quite an amazing sight!

When it's hungry for insects, its favorite food, a mudskipper approaches a limb or tree trunk.

It pulls itself up the trunk with its front fins and holds on with its back fins. It is able to climb a short distance up the tree. These fish also "skip" along the mudflats as they move from one tree to another. By quickly pushing their tails against the sand or mud, mudskippers can travel quite rapidly across the beach.

Although mudskippers spend a lot of time out of the water, they need to keep their skin moist. Occasionally, they will hop off their branches, walk across the sand, and jump into small tidal pools to wet their skin. Mudskippers need to keep their eyes wet, too. To do that, they often pull their eyes back into their head (they don't have tear ducts like you). Mudskippers' eyes can move in all directions—searching for insects while watching for other fish that might invade their territory.

Mudskippers are also unusual because they are one of the few fish able to breathe on land as well as in the water. In the water, mudskippers use their gills just like other fish. This allows them to take in oxygen from the surrounding water. On land, mudskippers are able to breathe because of a special series of membranes lining the back of their mouths and throats. These membranes are richly supplied with a network of blood vessels, allow-

ing mudskippers to absorb oxygen directly from the air. A fish that can breathe oxygen and walk up the trunks of trees is an example of adaptation—a physical feature or behavioral trait that has changed over time to improve an organism's chance for survival. The wide variety of plants and animals with which we live and the uncommon ways they live are exciting areas for exploration.

Fantastic Fact

In one species of mudskipper, the male fish do "push-ups" on the sand with their pectoral fins. This helps them attract females.

Millipedes are some of the most ancient of land animals. Most millipedes are small (about 1 inch or so) and are brown or black. Other varieties are large and come in a rainbow of colors, including red and orange. They can be found inside houses, under rocks, in cracks, and in leaf mold. They don't like light so they prefer to hide in dark places. Millipedes are found throughout the world.

Lots O' Legs

How would you walk if you had eight legs? How about 80 legs? How about 200 legs? How would you coordinate all those legs so that you could be able to move forward and not trip over a dozen or more of your own legs?

The millipede is a remarkable animal simply because of all its legs. The word millipede actually means thousand-footed, but no millipede has 1,000 feet. There are about 7,500 species of millipedes throughout the world. Some have as few as 20 legs, while a few tropical species have as many as 230 legs.

Oddly enough, most millipedes are clumsy and slow. Their legs are designed for moving through loose soil and humus (decaying matter on the ground) rather than scurrying out in the open. They are more at home pushing their way through the top layers of dirt and soil. Some millipedes however, are predators (animals that hunt and eat other animals). They can move rapidly when attacking their prey.

Because centipedes also have a lot of legs, many people confuse millipedes with centipedes, when in fact, they are not related at all. Centipedes (often referred to as "hundred-leggers") have one pair of legs per body segment and typically move in an S-shaped pattern. Millipedes, with two pairs of legs on each body segment, move in a straight line without wiggling.

Centipedes also have longer legs than millipedes, with the legs in the back longer than those in the front. The legs of millipedes are all the same size. Even though millipedes have many more legs than centipedes, they walk much slower.

Millipedes have round heads with a pair of short antennae. When disturbed, they coil up into a tight protective ball so that their enemies cannot get at them.

Several varieties of tropical millipedes give off a foul odor when they are disturbed. They do this through a series of stink glands located along both sides of their bodies. The fluid produced by these glands can, in some species, be sprayed for a distance of more than 2 feet. The fluid contains cyanide, a poison that temporarily blinds or injures any enemy seeking to make the millipede a meal. The millipede then has time to escape into the soil or surrounding plant life.

One species of tropical millipede grows up to 11 inches long. When it is disturbed it coils up into a ball the size of a golf ball.

About 500 species of tree frogs live in the tropics. North America has about 26 species, including the northern and southern cricket frogs, the California tree frog, the giant tree frog, and the spring peeper. Tree frogs can be found on every continent except Antarctica.

Twig Travelers

Walk through any tropical rain forest in Central or South America and look up in the branches of the overhanging trees. If you look carefully you may be able to locate some of the prettiest and most distinctive inhabitants of this ecosystem—tree frogs.

Tree frogs spend their entire lives in trees, seldom coming down to the ground. In fact, they eat, sleep, travel, and even lay their eggs high up in the branches of trees. Generally small with slender legs, they have sticky round toe pads on their feet which allow them to walk over, under, around, and upside down through the branches and leaves of rain forest trees. Their toe pads are so sticky that a tree frog can walk straight up a sheet of glass!

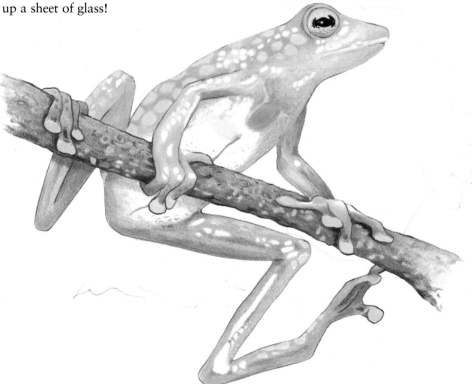

We often think of frogs as good leapers and jumpers; however, tree frogs walk much better than they can jump. The only time they do jump is when an unsuspecting insect or other tasty morsel flies by.

Tree frogs come in all colors of the rainbow. European frogs are green, strawberry-poison-dart frogs are red, banana tree frogs are brown, yellow reed frogs are yellow, and poison-dart frogs are blue. There's even a tree frog that is transparent—the glass frog. You can see right through its skin and watch its heart beat!

One of the best known tree frogs of the rain forest is the red-eyed tree frog. This colorful creature is nocturnal, awake and hunting during the night and sleeping during the day. Its most distinguishing feature is its big red eyes, which it uses to seek out food during its nightly hunts. It's also noted for laying its eggs under leaves that

Fantastic Fact

Frogs do not drink water— they absorb it through their skin.

hang out over small ponds or streams. As the eggs hatch, the tadpoles fall into the water below. There, they develop into frogs. Then, they will walk straight up into the trees where they spend the remainder of their lives.

One of the well-known tree frogs in the United States is the common gray tree frog. This frog has an ability to change color depending on its surroundings. Like a chameleon, the cells of its skin move, making the color change. If it is walking along green plants, its skin will be green. If it is resting or crawling on the bark of a tree, its skin will turn brown. Often called a "tree toad" its small size (1 to 2 inches) and coloring makes it difficult to locate.

OSTRICHES

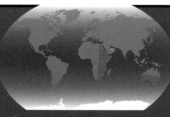

Rapid Runners

Ostriches can be found principally in eastern Africa and a few places in southern Australia. They enjoy living in dry areas and will often move about in large groups. In desert areas, they get their water by eating succulent plants. They also eat large amounts of sand to help them digest their food. Despite what many people think, they do not hide their heads in the sand.

Birds are animals that fly through the air with the greatest of ease. Eagles swoop and dive from great distances, sea gulls soar lazily over ocean waves, and robins dart through the trees around our homes. But have you ever seen a bird that *cannot* fly—a bird that spends its entire life walking or running—never flying?

Fantastic Fact

More than 5,000 hummingbird eggs (the world's smallest eggs) can fit inside *one* ostrich egg—the world's largest egg.

Ostriches are part of a group of birds known as flightless birds. These include Australian emus, New Guinea cassowaries, and New Zealand kiwis. Flightless birds make up less than 1 percent of all the birds in the world, but they also represent one-third of the 75 or more bird species that have become extinct (they no longer exist) over the past 400 years.

Ostriches are the world's tallest birds—males often grow to heights of 9 feet (half of that height is the bird's neck). Ostriches may weigh up to 330 pounds or more. Yet, in spite of their size, these birds are fast runners.

An adult ostrich can run as fast as 45 mph, but will often "cruise" at a steady speed of 31 mph over long stretches of flat land. Newborn ostrich chicks can run soon after they hatch. In a month, they can reach speeds of up to 35 mph.

When ostriches are chased by other animals, they don't run away. For some unknown reason, they just run around in a circle. If caught, ostriches will fight with their feet, both of which have two strong toes. The longest toe on each foot is armed with a sharp claw that can quickly injure any attacking enemy.

Ostriches like to mingle with other animals such as zebras and antelopes.

These animals kick up insects and other small animals that the ostriches like to eat. Because the ostriches are so tall, they can see approaching enemies and sound an "alarm" for their companions. By living together, several different animals can benefit one another.

Female ostriches lay 6 to 8 eggs at one time. Each of these eggs is 6 inches long and may weigh up to 2 pounds.

During the day, the female ostriches sit on the eggs. At night, the males incubate the eggs (keep them warm). After hatching, baby ostriches grow rapidly, reaching a height of 6 feet in six months.

Although ostriches cannot fly, they can travel faster than many other types of birds. This ability helps the ostrich live in its environment and escape from its enemies. It's one way the ostrich has been able to adapt to its surroundings.

Hydras can be found throughout the world, with about ten species living in the United States. Tan, gray, or brown in color, they are related to jellyfish, sea anemones, and corals. One species of hydra—*Chlorohydra viridissima*—has single-celled algae living in its cells, giving the hydra its greenish color.

Tumbling Tentacles

It's a flower that stings! It's a creature that eats its victims whole! And it's an organism that somersaults across the floor of a pond! What is it? A hydra.

Hydras can be found growing on sticks, stones, or water plants in all types of freshwater. Shaped like thin cylinders, they are approximately 1/4 to 1/2 inch long. At first glance, they look more like flowers than animals. One end of a hydra is surrounded by five to seven **tentacles** (long, thin arms), which can stretch out to make the hydra look like a long thread or pull back so that the hydra looks like a small egg.

Primarily, hydras use their tentacles to capture and eat small water creatures. Each tentacle has tiny cells that contain stinging threads. The threads are driven into an unsuspecting animal and a poison is released that paralyzes the victim. The entire meal is slowly pulled into the hydra's mouth to be digested whole.

Although hydras usually stay attached in one place for long periods of time, they also "walk" across the floor of a lake. To do this the hydra leans over and grips the surface with its tentacles. Then it somersaults into a new position. Can you imagine walking to school by somersaulting all the way there?

Hydras can reproduce through a process known as budding. From time to time small knobs appear on the surface of a hydra. As the buds grow, they begin to develop tentacles. When completely developed, the new organism breaks off and begins its life as an independent creature.

Although hydras have an unusual way of "walking," this method of locomotion helps them survive in their environment. In moving about, hydras can locate new sources of food as well as new areas in which to live.

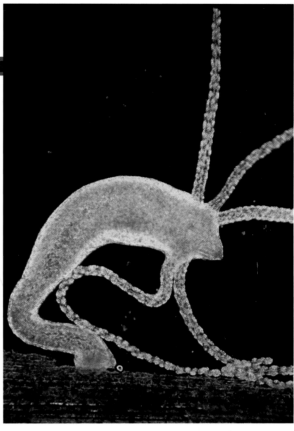

Hydras can regenerate (re-grow) and replace all their body cells in a period of several weeks.

Inching Insects

There are thousands of species of measuring worms found throughout the United States and Canada, and Europe and Asia. There are about 1,200 species just in the United States. While many species, such as cankerworms, damage fruit and shade trees, others, such as cabbage loopers, are responsible for serious damage to vegetables and other crops.

Here's an animal that not only walks strangely, it stands still in an unusual way, too. Some people call it a measuring worm, others refer to it as an inchworm, looper, or spanworm. But whatever name it goes by, it certainly travels in a distinctive manner.

If you look closely at a measuring worm, the first thing you notice is that it doesn't have any legs in the middle of its body. It has three pairs of tiny legs called prolegs on the front of its body and two or three sets of prolegs on the rear of its body. When it walks along a branch, it pulls the back part of its body up toward the front part, creating a hump in the middle. Then it grasps the surface of the branch tightly with its rear legs and extends the front part forward. It holds onto the surface with its front legs, releases its back legs, and humps up its middle—beginning the process all over again. When a measuring worm goes out for a walk, it looks like it is "inching" along, or carefully measuring the surface on which it walks. This is how it got its name.

Not only is the measuring worm a weird walker, it is also a "weird stander." Whenever a measuring worm feels threatened by an enemy, it "locks" itself into an upright position and remains motionless on a twig. It looks exactly like part of a twig or branch, standing still for hours until the danger passes. In fact, you could look right at a measuring worm and never notice it was a live animal. Measuring worms eat lots of vegetation—especially the leaves of trees. Thus, they are a serious pest of fruit farmers. After a measuring worm has finished its meal in one tree, it will quickly drop down from the branches of that tree on a long silken thread. The thread is spun in a manner similar to that of silkworms. Special glands near the worm's lower jaw give off a fluid that hardens into a fine thread as soon as it hits the air. One end of the thread is fastened to a branch or twig and the worm slides down this "ladder" to the ground. When it reaches the ground it will "inch" along to other vegetation or another tree to begin eating again.

Fantastic Fact

A measuring worm spends much of its life eating and will consume its own weight in leaves in a single day.

Creeping Crawlers

Mangrove trees can be found throughout Florida and other tropical areas. Dense thickets of mangrove trees are found at the mouths of rivers, in tidal creeks, and along shorelines. The trunk of the mangrove tree may reach 2 feet in diameter. They can grow as high as 80 feet in the tropics, while in Florida they grow to about 20 feet in height.

Plants can't walk, right? Well, technically, plants can't really walk, because walking means the ability to propel oneself by physically moving one or more body parts, usually the feet. And since most plants are firmly anchored into the ground by roots, they can't really walk like an insect or a frog or you. But let's meet a plant many people refer to as the "walking tree"—the mangrove tree.

A mangrove tree doesn't grow on land, but in shallow water along the shoreline. It does, however, help create land in several unusual ways. First, the mangrove tree is able to bloom throughout the year— its seeds appearing up and down its branches. Second, a root begins to grow from each seed while it's still on the tree. These roots may often grow to 1 foot in length. Eventually the seeds drop off the tree and into the surrounding water. The seeds may float away during high tide or stick into the mud during periods of low tide. Soon a new tree begins to grow, sending out spidery prop roots from its stem. In fact, a mangrove tree looks like a tall bush

Under the proper conditions, the "legs" of a mangrove tree can grow as fast as 1 inch every hour— that's two feet a day!

with many spidery legs sticking out in all directions.

As the roots of several mangrove trees grow, they become entangled with one another. Sand and dirt become trapped in the roots and soil begins to build up around them. Eventually, so much sand and mud form around the many roots that the tree is no longer in the water—it's on land!

Areas of mangrove trees are an important habitat for a wide variety of wildlife. Small fish, crabs, and other marine organisms use the roots as their home and as a place to obtain the food they need to survive. Birds use mangrove trees to build their nests and raise their young. Mangrove trees also prevent excessive loss of shorelines and beaches. By holding in the sand and

mud, they help reduce the amount of shoreline erosion (land that is worn and washed away) caused by waves, tides, and storms.

Mangrove trees never stop growing and they are continually spreading. Many mangrove seeds float to new areas, take root, and start new "islands." They continue to send out their spidery roots, making it seem as though whole groves of trees are "walking" out to sea. If you could take a series of photographs over a period of several months, you would be able to see how mangrove trees "walk" across large stretches of shallow water.

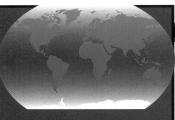

Sea Strollers

In some parts of the world, starfish are a major ecological problem. Since they enjoy eating mollusks, such as coral, they can be found in great numbers throughout the world and along many of the world's most beautiful coral reefs, such as the Great Barrier Reef of Australia. There, they are destroying large sections of the reef. Portions of this reef, which have been built up over hundreds of years, are being forever lost to starfish.

Found in all the oceans of the world, starfish are some of nature's most incredible creatures. There are more than 5,000 species of starfish—with some of the most unusual found in tropical waters. Starfish can have as few as four arms or as many as 50. At the end of each arm is a small red "eye" that is only able to sense light and dark. Starfish will range in size from as small as 1/2 inch across to others 3 feet in diameter.

Starfish move by means of numerous **tube feet** located on the underside of each arm. The tube feet are hollow muscular cylinders filled with water. When starfish walk, the "feet" are pushed out hydraulically by the contraction of muscular sacs. At the tips of the feet are suction discs which help starfish stick to rocks or prey. Starfish walk by fixing their suckers to the rocks and then pulling themselves forward.

In several species, one of the starfish's arms nearly always takes the lead when the starfish is walking. In other species, it is more usual for the arms to "take turns" in leading the way. The typical speed for a starfish is about 2 to 3 inches a minute.

One amazing feature of the starfish is its ability to regenerate lost arms. If an arm is pulled off or is damaged in some way, the starfish can grow a new arm over a period of several weeks. Some starfish can lose all their arms but one and not only survive, but regenerate all the missing arms.

Even though starfish do not have any teeth, they are **carnivorous** animals

Fantastic Fact

The Linckia starfish is able to pull itself in separate directions until it breaks into two parts. Each of the two parts can grow into a new animal.

(meat-eaters). Typically, they feed on clams, mollusks, worms, crustaceans, oysters, and fish. Shellfish are their favorite food, however. They eat clams and oysters by positioning themselves over the shell of their meal. Gripping a nearby rock with some of their suckers, they hold on to both halves of the oyster's or clam's shell with other suckers. Then they begin to pull the

two shell halves apart. Because of the clam's strong muscles, a starfish may need to pull for several hours or even several days before it can separate the shell halves. The starfish then pushes its stomach into the shellfish, inserting it inside out. The starfish secretes digestive juices into the unlucky mollusk and digests it right inside its own shell. Starfish are one of the few animals that can push their stomachs out of their bodies and turn them inside out to eat a meal. How do you think you would look with your stomach outside your body?

BASILISK LIZARDS

Basilisk lizards are found in Central and South America. The big feet and great speed of this lizard enable it to run across rivers, streams, and ponds. Many of the native peoples of the tropics call it the "Jesus Christ" lizard because of its ability to walk on water. Not only can the Basilisk lizard race on the water, it can run with great speed over the ground and through the treetops, too.

Water Walkers

Think about some of the places you walk—on sidewalks, on the playground, down dirt trails, or through the woods. All of those places are on land. What do you think would happen if you decided to walk on water? You'd quickly sink, that's what!

When we think about organisms that walk, we usually think about creatures that walk over land or through the trees. Few of us would ever think about an animal that walks on water. Yet, the basilisk lizard of Central and South America does just that!

The basilisk lizard lives near ponds and streams in tropical rain forests (dense, green forests with lots of rain, mostly in South America). Approximately 2 feet long, it has a large crest that runs from its head down the length of its body. From the side, it looks like an angry dragon. In fact, it was named for an ancient Greek monster that breathed fire and poison. Legends told of how people died after one glance from its fearsome eyes.

When a basilisk lizard is disturbed by an enemy, it drops down from the trees where it lives into the water below. It begins to move its back feet rapidly and, by holding its body semi-erect, is able to run across the surface of the water without falling in. It can do this because its body is lightweight and its hind legs are long and thin and end in toes fringed with scales. Although its back feet look like those of a frog, they are not webbed. Strong muscles help the basilisk move the rear legs so rapidly that the soles of its feet do not break through the water surface when it runs.

After the basilisk has run across the surface of a pond or stream for one to three dozen yards, it begins to slow down and eventually sinks into the water. There, it is able to continue its journey by quickly swimming to the opposite shore.

The ability of the basilisk to run across the surface of water helps it survive in its natural environment. It is also how this amazing animal has learned to adapt to its surroundings.

Slimy Slippers

Most of the animals you know have two or four or eight feet. That is, all of their feet come in pairs. You're about to meet an animal that has only one foot and that foot is actually its stomach!

The snail is a most amazing creature. It is one member of a group of animals called **gastropods,** or "bellyfoots." That means that these animals travel around on their stomachs. How would you like to spend the day crawling around on your stomach?

When a snail "walks" it moves by generating a series of waves along the length of its foot. These waves pass from the front to the back of the foot creating a rippling motion. Also, as it moves, the snail gives out a slimy substance from just behind its head. This slime helps it travel over rough surfaces and sharp objects. In fact, a snail can climb over a razor blade without cutting itself! The slime track that the snail creates is not a continuous smear, however, but actually a series of patches where sections of the foot have come in contact with the ground.

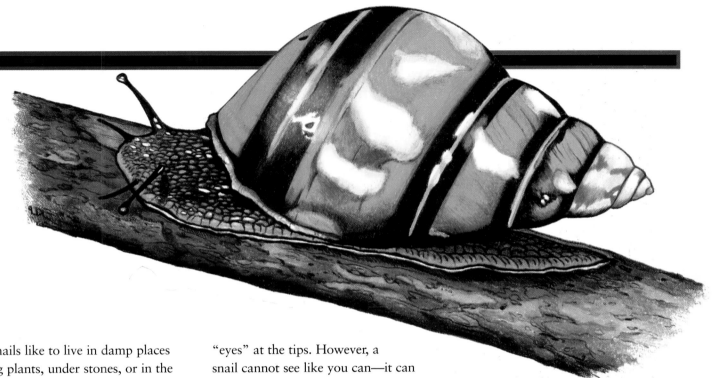

Snails like to live in damp places among plants, under stones, or in the soil. They are most active when the weather is wet or moist. In dry weather, snails are often inactive and may attach themselves to a wall or tree trunk and withdraw into their shells for a period of several days or weeks.

This brief period of inactivity is called estivation and is similar to hibernation—the time when snails bury themselves under several inches of soil, slow down their bodily functions, and remain inactive over the cold winter months. In very dry areas or very cold areas of the world, some snails are able to hibernate for up to four years!

A snail has two sets of tentacles. The upper pair is longer and have "eyes" at the tips. However, a snail cannot see like you can—it can only tell light from dark. The other set of tentacles is much shorter, and they are used to feel objects as the snail walks along. These tentacles are also used to "hear" sounds by detecting vibrations of objects or organisms. Both sets of tentacles can be pulled into the head of the snail whenever it feels threatened or wants to protect itself.

An animal that can walk on one foot! An animal whose one foot is actually its stomach! An animal whose head is on its foot! Truly, the snail is a most amazing walker—one you are sure to discover in your garden or in some nearby woods.

Snails have up to 20,000 little teeth— all on their tongues.

Pond Patrols

Usually less than 1 inch in length and with a slender body, these long-legged bugs can be found in freshwater areas all over the world. There are about 30 species of water striders in North America.

To find food, to seek a mate, or to escape from their enemies, many animals need to travel from one place to another. To do this, most animals live in specialized locations. One of the more distinctive is an animal that spends most of its life living and walking on the surface of water—water striders.

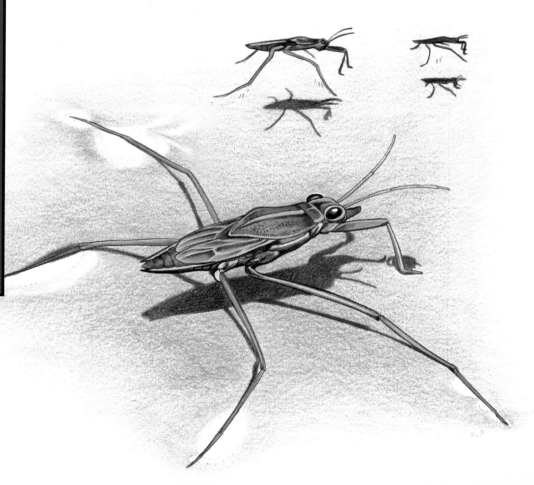

If you have ever visited a pond or looked carefully at a slow-moving stream, you may have seen these creatures darting about on the surface of the water. In fact, these insects are able to run, walk, skip, and hop all over the surface of the water without ever getting wet.

Water striders have three pairs of legs; however, they only use the back four feet when they walk on the water. These two pairs of legs have thick pads of hair on them that repel water and prevent water striders from sinking. The back legs are used to steer water striders across the surface of the water, while the middle legs are used to push them along.

Typically, water striders congregate in large numbers on the surface of the water. Here, they feed on smaller insects or other invertebrates (animal that don't have backbones). Water striders are predatory animals, attacking other creatures and using their sharp piercing mouthparts to suck the body fluids from their prey.

Although water striders can easily walk across the surface of a pond, they are also great runners. They can move at great speeds over the surface of the water. Whole groups of them skipping across the surface of a pond is truly an amazing sight.

Water striders are also known for leaping into the air and landing softly on the surface of the water without getting wet. Unfortunately, all this movement tends to attract the attention of fish who like to sneak up from below to make a tasty meal of these water walkers.

Fantastic Fact

When walking, water striders hold their short front legs up under their heads for balance. Their bodies never touch the water.

The sloth is a mammal found deep in the rain forests of Central and South America. There are seven species of sloths divided into two groups—the two-toed sloths and the three-toed sloths. Two-toed sloths can be found from Honduras to Northern Argentina. Three-toed sloths can be found from Venezuela to Brazil. The two-toed sloth is more common than the three-toed sloth and is the type most often seen in zoos.

Careful Creepers

You have met some animals that can walk on water, others that can walk on their stomachs, and even some animals that can walk with no legs at all! But have you ever met an animal that can walk upside down?

One of the most unusual animals in the world, the sloth spends almost its entire life upside down. The sloth not only walks upside down through the trees, it also sleeps, mates, and gives birth to its babies while it hangs upside down. In fact, sloths may sleep for more than 20 hours a day hanging from the branches of a tree.

A sloth "walks" slowly through a tree and is one of the slowest moving animals in the world. The average "speed" for a sloth is about 4 feet a minute. Many people often refer to something that is slow moving as "slothful."

Sloths belong to the order of animals known as Edentata, which means "without teeth." It was once thought that sloths had no teeth, but they do have a set of black teeth which are difficult to see from a distance. They use these teeth to eat leaves and fruit in the trees where they live.

Sloths hang from the rain forest trees by means of long curved claws that look like meat hooks. Their arms are much longer than their legs and are ideally suited for an upside-down life. Unfortunately, sloths cannot walk upright on their arms and legs. Whenever they are on the ground they must slowly (and painfully) drag themselves to another tree.

Another distinguishing feature of sloths not found in any other animal is the fact that their hair grows from their bellies to their backs. In most mammals, hair grows from the top of the back to the stomach. But because sloths live upside down in a very wet environment, their "opposite-growing" hair allows rainwater to run off. Sloth hair is also covered by a layer of green algae (aquatic plant organisms) which helps conceal them from enemies. Their green color and sluggish habits make sloths look more like masses of dead leaves than living animals.

The enemies of sloths include jaguars and ocelots, as well as the most dangerous enemy of all—humans. The native peoples of the rain forests hunt sloths for their meat. Other people are burning down large sections of rain forests destroying the plants that sloths need to survive. As the rain forest is destroyed, so is the habitat of the sloth. There may come the day when the only sloths alive will be those found in zoos.

Fantastic Fact

The fastest recorded speed for a three-toed sloth is .068 mph—that's only 6 feet per minute!

PROTECTING WEIRD WALKERS

The following groups and organizations have lots of information you can use. Call or write them and ask for material on how you can become involved in preserving plant and animal species around the world.

Save the Rain Forest

604 Jamie Street
Dodgeville, WI 53533
(Raises money to purchase and preserve large tracts of rain forest land and works with native peoples to protect the plants and animals of the rain forest, including sloths, tree frogs, and basilisk lizards.)

National Wildlife Federation

8925 Leesburg Pike
Vienna, VA 22184
(Works to preserve, conserve, and properly manage plant and wildlife resources around the world.)

The animals and plants you read about in this book are examples of organisms with unusual means of locomotion. Their means of travel is a factor in how they are able to survive in a particular environment. Creatures that run fast (basilisk lizards, ostriches) are able to escape from their enemies. Slow-moving animals (sloths, snails) can conserve their energy while locating food.

The ways in which an organism travels through its environment is an example of adaptation—features or behaviors that help an organism survive in a particular environment over a period of years. Organisms adapt to their environments by learning about which foods to eat, who their enemies are, and how to travel through that environment. Adaptation is a process that may take hundreds or thousands of years. It is not something that happens quickly.

Unfortunately, something that does happen quickly is the destruction of certain environments around the world. When humans burn down large sections of the Brazilian rain forest, part of the sloth's environment is endangered. When people drain shorelines and fill them in to build housing developments, part of the mangrove tree's environment is endangered. When farmers spray dangerous chemicals or pesticides on their fields, the millipede's environment is endangered. For many organisms it may have taken hundreds of years to adapt to a particular environment. Yet, that environment can be destroyed or seriously altered in just a few years, resulting in the death or elimination of large numbers of plants and animals.

As you might suspect, humans are the major cause of the extinction of many organisms. The eradication of habitats, the depletion of food sources, and the introduction of foreign species into an area all contribute to this global problem. But that does not mean that we can't all work together to reduce this dilemma.

I invite you to join with your teachers, parents, and friends and work together so that the weird walkers and other inhabitants of this planet will be around for many years and many generations. First of all, take some time to learn about the organisms that live in your part of the world. You may wish to read other books like this one or talk with various adults (such as a high school biology teacher or a college professor) to discover information about the plants and animals native to your area.

Another way you can learn more about various organisms is to visit nearby botanical gardens, zoos, wildlife preserves, aquariums, and arboretums. Be sure to share what you discover with family members and classmates. Also, you may wish to write to various conservation groups (see the list on these pages) and ask them for informational brochures or newsletters. By learning as much as possible and getting involved, we can all help preserve the weird walkers of the world as well as other plants and animals. Together, we can make a difference!

National Audubon Society

666 Pennsylvania Avenue SE
Washington, DC 20003
(A strong advocate of environmental protection, this group helps pass environmental laws, maintains national sanctuaries and nature centers, and conducts a variety of educational programs for adults and kids.)

The Nature Conservancy

1815 N. Lynn Street
Arlington, VA 22209
(Its mission is to purchase selected habitats around the world—thus protecting the plant life and animals that live in those distinctive environments.)

Friends of Wildlife Conservation

New York Zoological Society
185 Street, Southern Blvd.
Bronx Zoo
Bronx, NY 10460
(This group works to ensure the survival of many animals around the world, including several endangered species.)

Many organisms have unusual means of locomotion. Just because an animal (or plant) is a "weird walker" doesn't mean we should treat it any differently from the other creatures of the world. What it does mean, however, is that there is a remarkable diversity of life on our planet—life that needs to be protected and preserved. Here's a list of other organisms that are weird walkers. Some of them may live near you; others may live in far distant countries.

HOUSEFLY

This common insect is able to walk upside down on ceilings because of a special balancing organ in back of its body.

WALKING CATFISH

This Florida fish "walks" from lake to lake using its fins as feet. It can stay out of water for two months or more.

ROBBER CRAB

These creatures use their long front claws to walk straight up the trunks of coconut trees.

DADDY LONG-LEGS

These insects walk with eight legs. They are able to break legs off when caught by enemies. If necessary, they can walk with only two legs.

WALKING STICK

This tropical insect looks like a small twig walking through the leaves of the forest floor.

MOLE CRAB

This creature, which lives along the seashore, always walks backward.

GRAY KANGAROO

This Australian animal walks through a series of jumps—each more than 11 feet high. Each hop can cover a length of 44 feet.

NEREIDS

When the moon is full, these segmented worms rise up out of the sand and dance across the beach. The dance ends when the worms explode into many pieces.

AMOEBA

These tiny creatures move by using "false feet"—jelly-like extensions that melt back into their bodies as soon as they move forward.

BLOWFLIES

When this fly walks, it is able to "smell" the surface with the fine hairs on its feet.